SCHOLASTIC

The Best of **NURSERY** education

Instant
photocopiables

Ages
3-5

▶ **Sequencing
activities**
▶ **Essential
templates**
▶ **Language
and maths**
▶ **Creative
ideas**

All the best activities from the UK's leading early years magazine

Editor
Susan Elliott

Designers
Andrea Lewis and Joy Monkhouse

Cover photograph
Ray Moller

Acknowledgement
Qualifications and Curriculum Authority for the use of extracts from the QCA/ DfEE document Curriculum Guidance for the Foundation Stage © 2000 Qualification and Curriculum Authority.

© 2005, Scholastic Ltd

Published by Scholastic Ltd, Villiers House, Clarendon Avenue, Leamington Spa, Warwickshire CV32 5PR.

Visit our website at www.scholastic.co.uk

Printed by Bell & Bain Ltd.

1 2 3 4 5 6 7 8 9 0   5 6 7 8 9 0 1 2 3 4

British Library Cataloguing-in-Publication Data. A catalogue record for this book is available from the British Library.

ISBN 0-439-96510-1
ISBN 9-780-439-96510-1

All articles previously published in *Nursery Education* magazine between September 2001 and June 2004 or specially commissioned for this book.
    The authors' rights have been asserted by them in accordance with the Copyright, Designs and Patents Act 1988.

Contents

Foreword

By Sue Owen, Director, Early Childhood Unit, National Children's Bureau.

Even the most well qualified, experienced and creative of professionals need a few fresh ideas from time to time.

Most early years practitioners take inspiration from the practical projects and themes provided, in abundance, by magazines aimed at our sector, and *Nursery Education's* are among the best.

A recent study on how early years practitioners access information, conducted by the National Children's Bureau, found that the majority of respondents relied on magazines for updates and tips as well as on their colleagues.

This series helpfully pulls together a collection of *Nursery Education's* projects, so you can find them all in one place.

Often the best ideas and projects arise out of children's own interests - many of which are reflected in this collection. The collection offers new ideas (and reminders for some trusted favourites which you may have forgotten) as springboards for your work.

Resources such as this are an ideal addition to team discussions. They can stimulate new thinking as well as bringing the knowledge of a wide range of early years experts to the table.

Thanks to *Nursery Education's* new resource collection, practitioners will now have access to a pool of information from colleagues across the country.

Introduction

If you are a regular subscriber to *Nursery Education*, you will already appreciate just what a versatile, time-saving resource the magazine is. Each issue contains all you need to deliver a themed project in your setting, plus essential information that enables you to keep up-to-date with current developments in the early years sector.

We have built on this successful formula and made it even better by selecting the very best activities and information from past issues of the magazine, and compiling them into a series of exciting new books.

In this book, you will find a collection of photocopiable activity sheets that provide fun opportunities to extend the children's learning across the curriculum. As well as maths games and language activities, we have included practical craft ideas plus some e activities and a selection of time-saving themed templates.

We have had great fun putting this new set of books together, and we hope you find them to be a valuable addition to your setting! If you would like more information on *Nursery Education*, please visit our website www.scholastic.co.uk, telephone: 0845 8504411 or see page 64 of this book.

Sarah Sodhi, Editor, *Nursery Education* magazine.

Chapter 1
Language activities

The activity sheets in this chapter have been specially selected to help your children to develop their language and communication skills. Use them to support your everyday activities to help reinforce and consolidate the children's learning, or as stand-alone sheets to develop specific skills.

Spiral shells

Start at the dots and follow the dotted lines to draw the snail shells. Colour in your picture.

Concept © Mavis Brown

Illustration © Gaynor Berry

Photocopiable

Colourful castle

Use coloured pens to follow the dotted lines on the giant's castle.

Concept © Jenni Tavener

Illustration © Gaynor Berry

Photocopiable

Alphabet letters

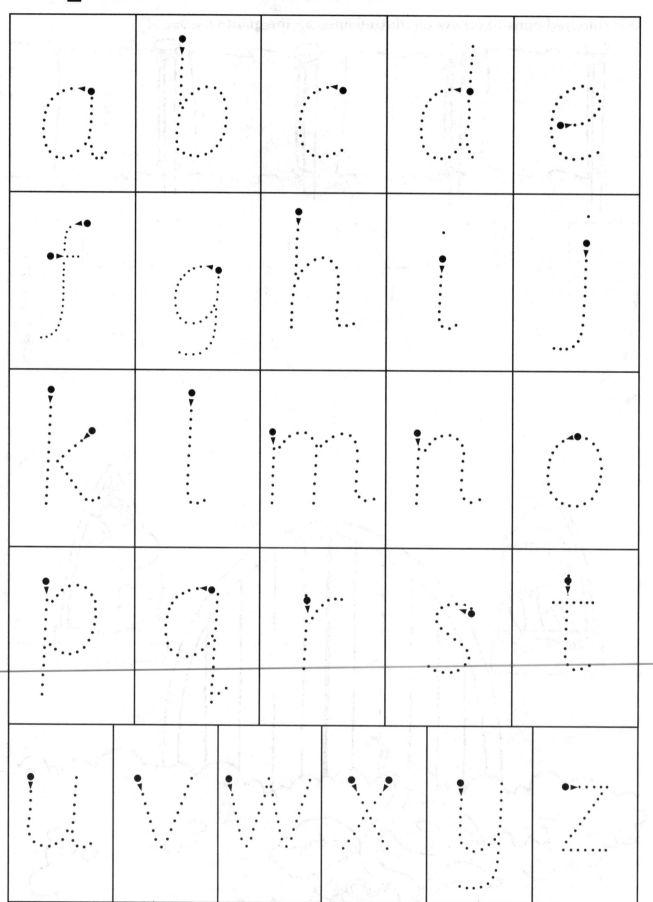

Photocopiable

Our pet shop

Cut out the pictures and match the pets to the correct initial letters.

Photocopiable

Illustration © Maureen Galvani

Colourful tents

Colour in each tent with a different colour starting with 'b', 'g' and 'p'.

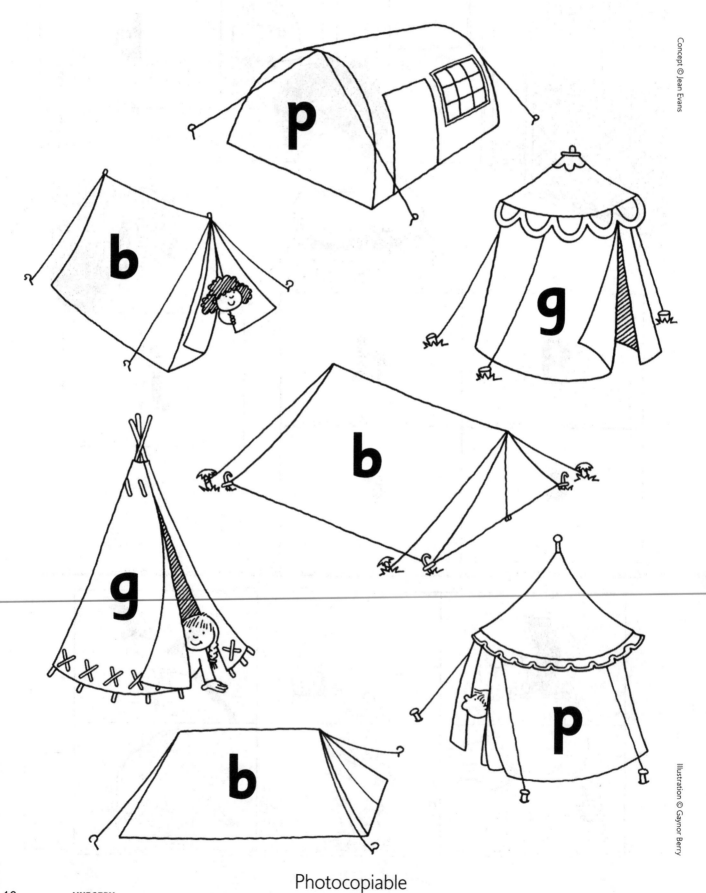

Concept © Jean Evans

Illustration © Gaynor Berry

Photocopiable

Butterfly trail

Use a pencil to follow the butterfly trail around the path. Say the names of the things that the butterfly sees. Draw lines to match the pictures with the letters that they begin with.

Concept © Brenda Williams

Illustration © Rebecca Finn

b	f	g	t

Photocopiable

Rhyming pets

Name the three pictures in each line. Colour in the pictures for the two objects that sound the same in each line. Put a cross through the object that does not rhyme.

Concept © Brenda Williams

Illustration © Maureen Galvani

Photocopiable

Odd one out

Say the name of each object in each box. Draw a circle around the object in each box that does not rhyme.

Photocopiable

Concept © Allison Hedley

Illustration © Gaynor Berry

Santa's poem

Write or draw three things that Santa might bring on Christmas Eve.

Santa has been and we can see...

_____

_____

and

_____

for you and me.

Photocopiable

Weather chart

Draw pictures or write words to show what the weather is like in the morning and afternoon.

Cloudy Sunny Rainy Windy

Concept © Barbara J Leach

	Morning	Afternoon
	🕛 O'clock	🕛 O'clock
Monday		
Tuesday		
Wednesday		
Thursday		
Friday		

Illustration © Gaynor Berry

Photocopiable

Best for baby

Draw lines to match the summer and winter clothes and objects to the correct babies.

Concept © Brenda Williams

Summer baby

Winter baby

Illustration © Baz Rowell

Photocopiable

Family figures

Think about your home and your family. Draw lines from the pictures to the person who usually does this job at home. You can draw more than one line from each picture.

me

Photocopiable

Who lives here?

Cut out the pictures and match the characters to their fantasy homes. Tell a story about each character and their home.

Concept © Brenda Williams

Illustration © Piers Harper

Photocopiable

Our local area

Go on a walk around your local area. What other types of home can you see? Tick the boxes as you find each type of home.

Concept © Maureen Warner

Illustration © Piers Harper

Photocopiable

Finish the words

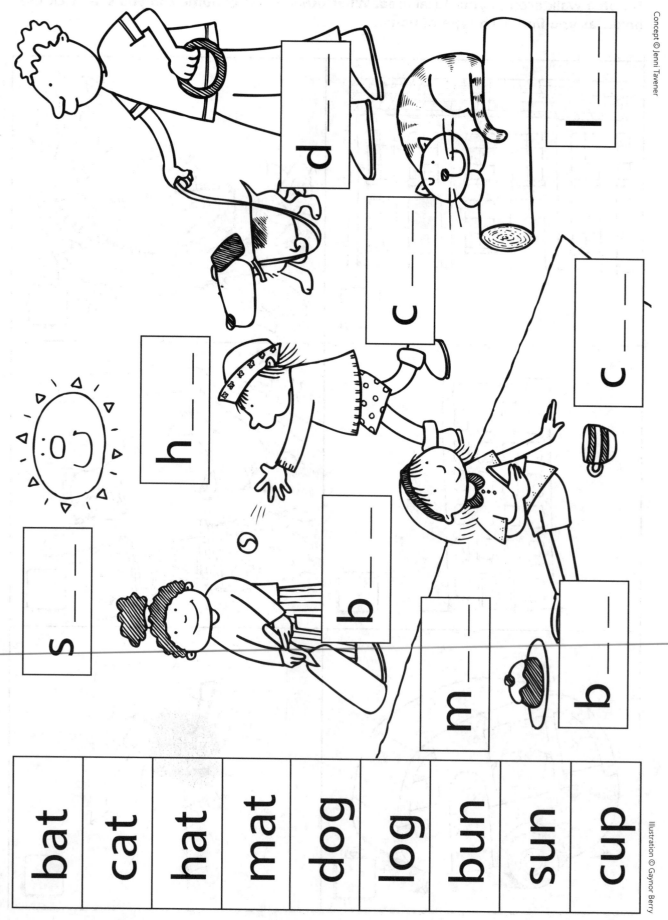

d — —

— — l

c — —

c — —

h — —

b — —

s — —

m — —

b — —

bat	cat	hat	mat	dog	log	bun	sun	cup

Concept © Jenni Tavener

Illustration © Gaynor Berry

Photocopiable

Chapter 2
Maths activities

From number formations to shape searches, counting games to positional and directional challenges, the games and activities in this chapter provide fun and exciting opportunities to help develop a broad range of mathematical skills for children of all abilities.

Numbers

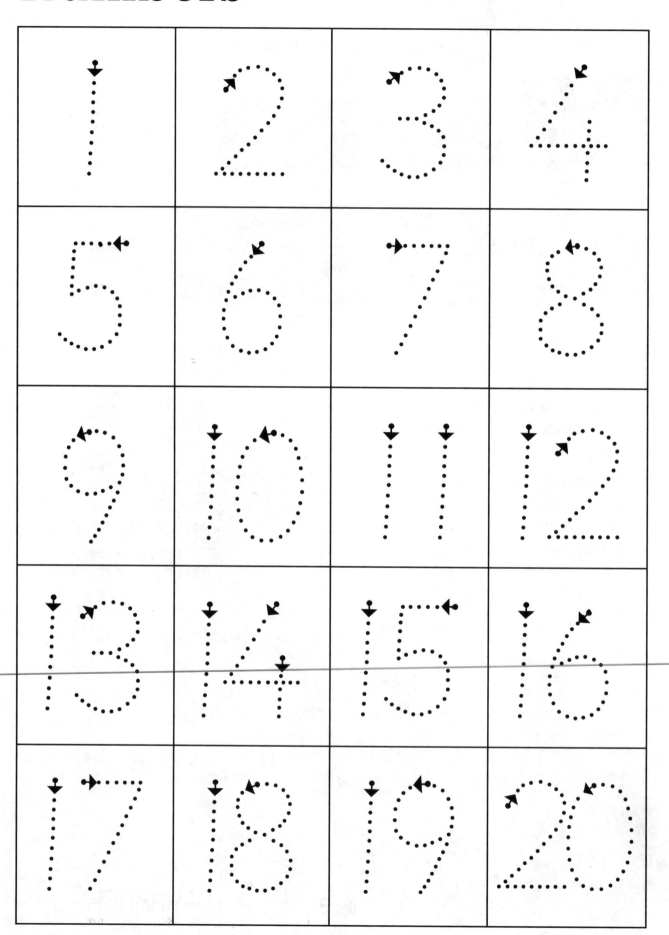

Photocopiable

Round the houses

Can you help the postperson to deliver the letters? Draw lines to match the letters to the houses with the same numbers. Colour in the houses.

Photocopiable

Concept © Sarah Dix

Illustration © Jenny Tulip

Winter store

The squirrels have hidden some acorns for winter. How many can you find? Write the number in the box at the bottom of the page. Number each acorn as you find it.

I found ☐ acorns

Photocopiable

Tunnels and trains

How many carriages are going in to each tunnel? Circle the correct numbers.

Photocopiable

The Best of **NURSERY** education

Concept © Joyce Lydford

Illustration © Gaynor Berry

Incy Wincy Spider

Count the raindrops and write the answers in the boxes.

1 2 3 4 5 6 7 8 9

Concept © Jenni Tavener

Illustration © Gaynor Berry

Photocopiable

Colourful creatures

Play this game in pairs or groups. Throw a colour dice and colour a minibeast. Use a different colour for each creature. The first person to colour in all six minibeasts is the winner!

Photocopiable

Concept © Jenni Tavener

Illustration © Gaynor Berry

Flower beetle game

Play this game in pairs or groups. Throw a dice to match the shapes and colour in the flower. The first person to complete the flower is the winner.

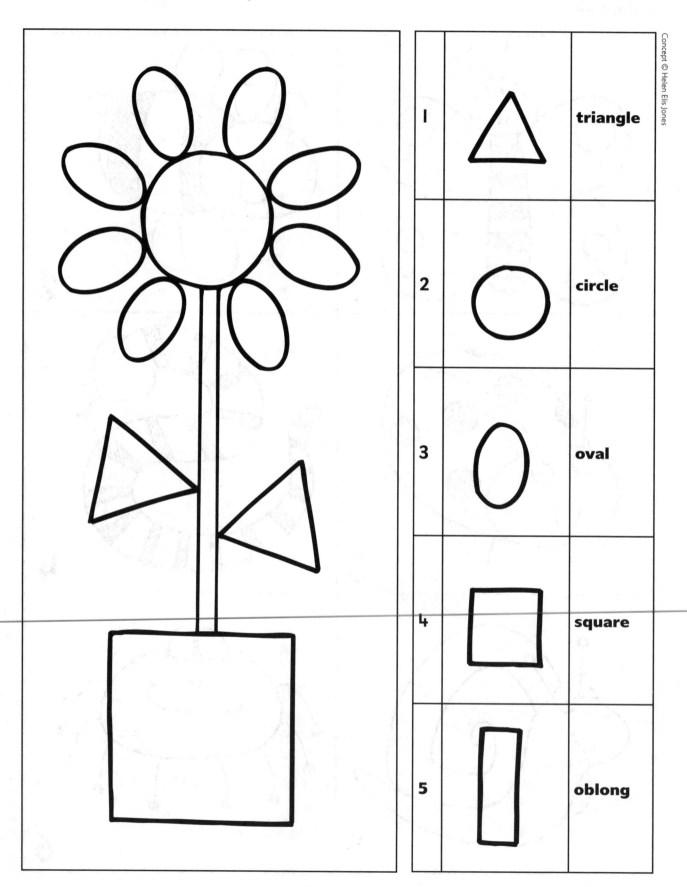

1	△	**triangle**
2	◯	circle
3	⬭	**oval**
4	☐	**square**
5	▯	**oblong**

Concept © Helen Ellis Jones

Photocopiable

Door to door

Play this game in pairs or groups. Use a dice and counters to move from house number 1 to house number 10 and back again. The first player to get back to house number 1 is the winner.

Concept © Joyce Lydford

Illustration © Piers Harper

Photocopiable

Beanstalk game

Play this game in pairs or groups. Throw two dice and add the numbers together to move up the beanstalk. The first to reach the finish is the winner.

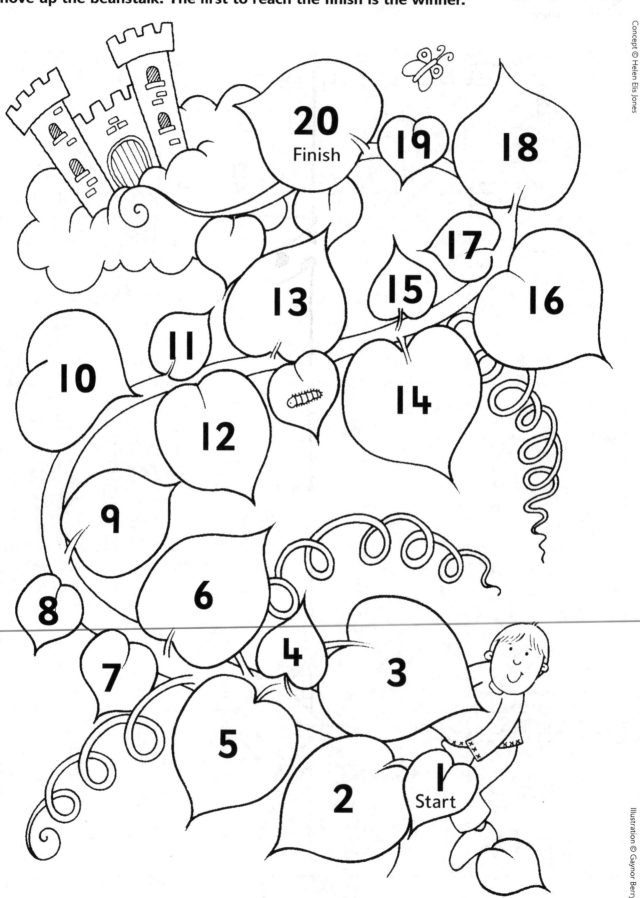

Photocopiable

Concept © Helen Elis Jones

Illustration © Gaynor Berry

Snakes and ladders

Play this game in pairs or groups. Take turns to roll a dice and move your counters. Climb up the ladders and slide down the snakes.

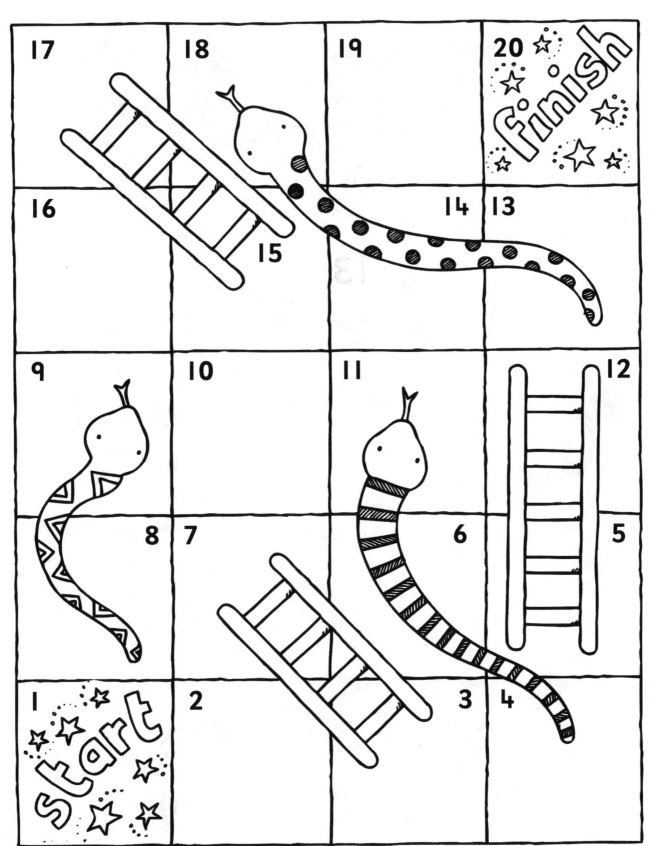

Patternpillars

Colour the patternpillars to make a recurring pattern then cut them out. Draw and cut out a leaf that is big enough for each caterpillar to fit on. Stick the caterpillars on to their leaves. Which is the bigger?

Concept © Kevin Kelman

Photocopiable

Friendship dominoes

Colour in and cut out the dominoes. Play the game with a friend.

Photocopiable

The Best of NURSERY education 33

Around the farmyard

How many different ways can the farmer go to feed each animal? Which animals does he pass?

Text © Jenni Tavener

Illustration © Gaynor Berry

Photocopiable

In the lounge

Look at the picture. What is happening? Talk about the different positions of the people and the objects.

Concept © Sally Gray

Illustration © Gaynor Berry

Photocopiable

Shape search

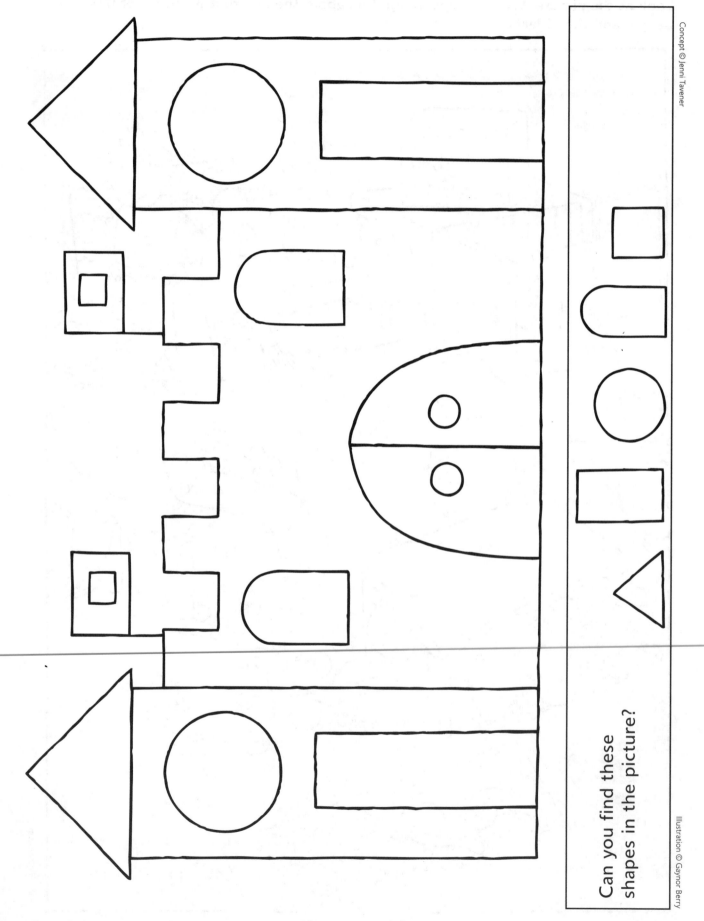

Can you find these shapes in the picture?

Concept © Jenni Tavener

Illustration © Gaynor Berry

Photocopiable

Chapter 3
Sorting and sequencing activities

The progressive activities in
this chapter will help children to
think logically about sequencing,
sorting and matching, and
explain the reasons for their
decisions. They can be used
for individual work or group
challenges to suit your own
children's needs.

Pot plants

Colour in, then cut out the drawings. Place them in the correct order to show how to sow seeds into a pot and how the seeds grow into flowers

Concept © Mavis Brown

Illustration © Louise Gardner

Photocopiable

Field to table

Colour in and cut out the pictures. Put them into the correct sequence to show how we get our daily bread.

The farmer grows the wheat.

The harvester cuts the wheat.

The miller grinds the grain.

The baker bakes the bread.

The family buys the bread.

The children eat the bread.

Concept © Judith Harries

Illustration © Gaynor Berry

Photocopiable

At the farm

Colour in and cut out the pictures. Put the pictures in order to tell a story. Can you write the story on a sheet of paper.

Concept © Barbara J Leach

Illustration © Sami Sweeten

Photocopiable

Panda's busy day

Colour in and cut out the pictures. Shuffle them and then arrange them in order to show Panda's day.

Concept © Hannah Mortimer

Illustration © Lynda Murray

Photocopiable

The Best of NURSERY education

Home sweet home

Say what you can see in each picture. Cut out the pictures and match the pets to their correct homes.

Photocopiable

Can we eat it?

Cut out the pictures and sort them into two piles – things that we can eat and things that we cannot eat.

Photocopiable

Find the pairs!

The shoemaker's shoes have got muddled. Can you find the pair of shoes on each shelf and colour them in?

Concept © Jenni Tavener

Illustration © Louise Gardner

Photocopiable

What comes next?

Look carefully at the patterns in each row. Cut out the four pictures at the bottom of the page. Find the correct picture to finish the pattern in each row.

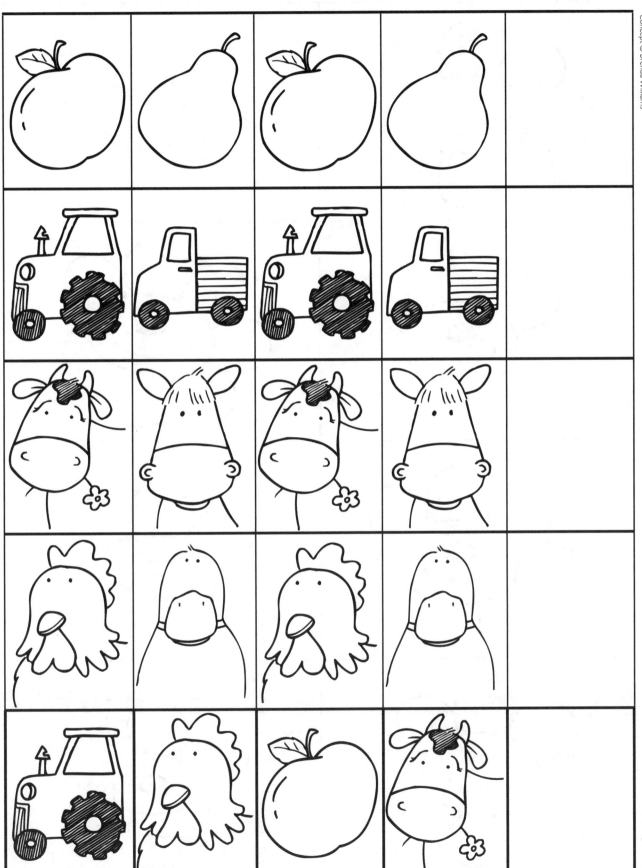

Concept © Brenda Williams

Illustration © Gaynor Berry

Photocopiable

Falling petals

Colour in the pictures and then cut them out. Put them into the correct sequence to show the flower losing its petals.

Concept © Jeni Tavener

Photocopiable

Chapter 4
Creative activities

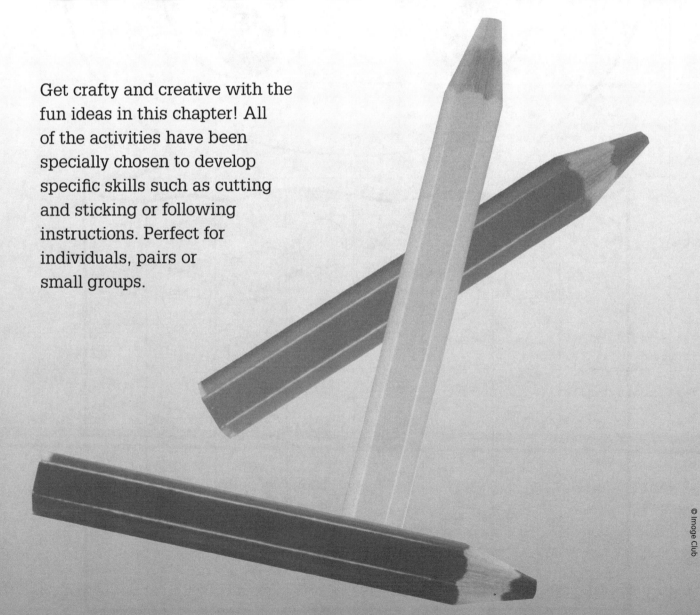

Get crafty and creative with the fun ideas in this chapter! All of the activities have been specially chosen to develop specific skills such as cutting and sticking or following instructions. Perfect for individuals, pairs or small groups.

Wobbly octopus

**Decorate the octopus' tentacles with glitter and sequins. Cut between each tentacle.
Thread some string through the hole and hang your octopus up.**

Concept © Kevin Kelman

Photocopiable

Tangram shapes

Colour in the shapes then cut along the lines. Rearrange them to make shapes and pictures. How many different pictures can you make?

Concept © Allison Hedley

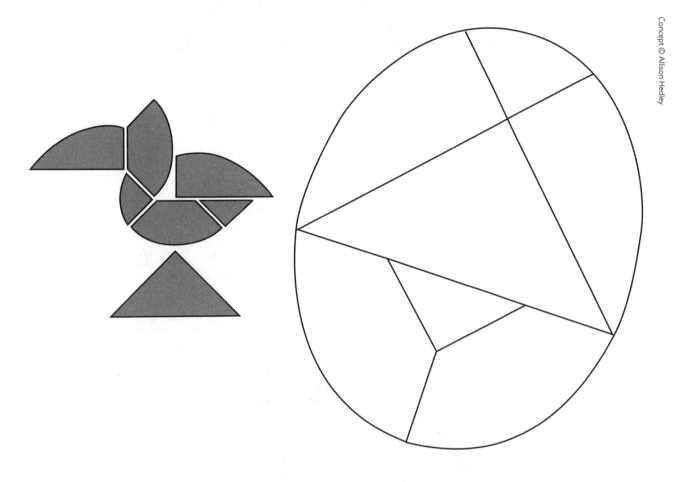

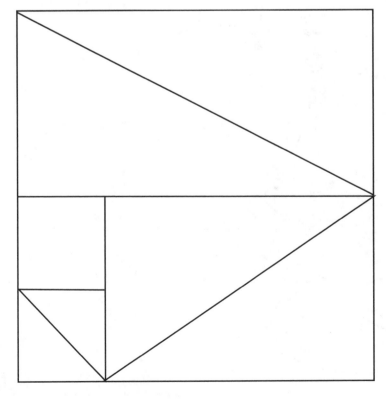

Photocopiable

Rainy day

Ask an adult to copy the picture on to card and punch a hole through each raindrop. Sew through the holes to make a rainy day picture.

Concept © Pauline Kenyon

Illustration © Gaynor Berry

Photocopiable

What shall I wear?

Cut out pictures of clothes for different types of weather and stick them on the figure.

Concept © Kevin Kelman

Illustration © Gaynor Berry

Photocopiable

Make a windmill

Concept © Jean Evans

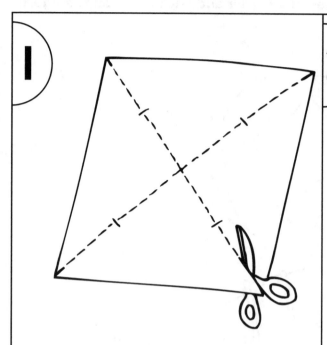

1

● Fold a 15cm square piece of paper twice diagonally to form a small triangle.
● Open the paper out.
● Mark a point on each fold, 8cm from the outer corner.
● Cut along the folds up to the marked point.

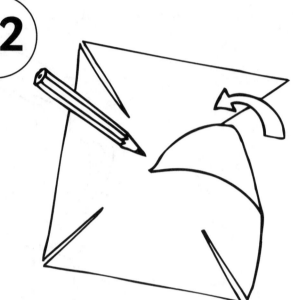

2

● Fold alternate halves of each corner into the centre of the square, slightly overlapping the centre point each time.
● Push a sharp pencil through the centre of the square to make a hole.

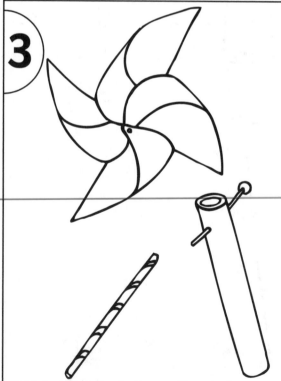

3

● Make two holes in the cardboard tube.
● Push a straw through the holes and ensure that it turns freely.
● Secure the straw at the back with a small lump of play dough.

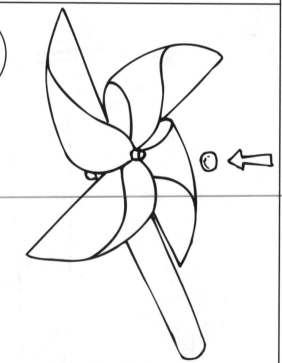

4

● Push the straw through the holes in the folded paper square.
● Trim off the excess straw at the front of the windmill.
● Secure at the front with another lump of play dough.

Illustration © Baz Rowell

Photocopiable

Origami doll

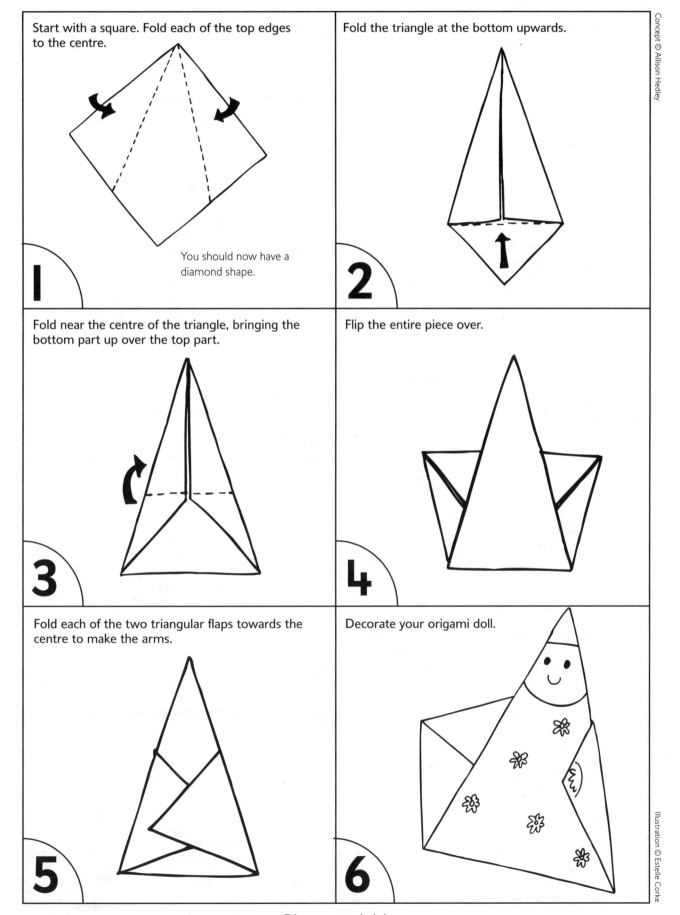

1 Start with a square. Fold each of the top edges to the centre.

You should now have a diamond shape.

2 Fold the triangle at the bottom upwards.

3 Fold near the centre of the triangle, bringing the bottom part up over the top part.

4 Flip the entire piece over.

5 Fold each of the two triangular flaps towards the centre to make the arms.

6 Decorate your origami doll.

Concept © Allison Hedley

Illustration © Estelle Corke

Photocopiable

Magic letters

Follow the instructions to make some tasty magic letters!

What you need: Ready-to-make bread mix; plastic mixing bowls; wooden spoons; oven-proof baking sheets; currants; measuring jug; small, clean table-cloth; water; aprons.

1 Put on aprons, roll up sleeves and wash hands.

2 Add water to the mix and knead for five minutes.

3 Roll out sausage shapes and shape into letters or spirals.

4 Cover with a small, clean table-cloth and leave in a warm spot.

5 After one hour, remove the table-cloth and see what has happened!

6 Place on a baking sheet and cook in a pre-heated oven (230°C/450°F/Gas Mark 8) for 15 to 20 minutes.

Remember to wash up and put away the equipment!

Illustration © Baz Rowell

Photocopiable

Cheese gems

You will need:
- 40g cheese
- 175g self raising flour
- 25g butter
- 100ml milk

- Oven (set at 220° C, 425° F/Gas Mark 7)
- Pastry cutters
- Wire rack
- Baking tray

Wash your hands

1 Rub flour and butter together.

2 Mix in cheese and milk.

3 Press into a soft dough.

4 Roll out on a floured board.

5 Cut with small cutters and place on a baking tray.

6 Bake for 7-8 minutes then cool on a wire rack.

Concept © Jenni Tavener

Illustration © Gaynor Berry

Photocopiable

Jack's salad

Work in a group to make a healthy salad for a picnic or for snack time.

Ingredients
- 1 crisp lettuce
- 10 cherry tomatoes
- 3 spring onions (optional)
- 5 eggs
- 1 tablespoon mayonnaise
- 2 teaspoons vinegar or lemon juice
- 3 tablespoons olive oil
- 450g French green beans
- 1 small tin cannellini beans, drained

What to do
- Place the eggs in a pan of cold water. Hardboil for 10 minutes then place in cold water to cool.
- Cut the tops and tails off the green beans and wash. Place in a pan of boiling water and cook for around 4 minutes until just tender. Drain and cool.
- Wash the lettuce. Pat dry with a tea towel. Tear into pieces.
- Wash and dry the tomatoes. Cut into quarters.
- Peel the eggs and cut into small pieces.
- Cut the beans into short lengths.
- Wash, dry and cut the onions into small pieces.
- Place all of these things in a large bowl with the cannellini beans.
- In a small bowl mix together the mayonnaise, vinegar and olive oil to make a dressing. Pour over the salad and mix gently with a spoon.
- Keep cool until ready to eat.

Concept © Liz Powlay

Illustration © Gaynor Berry

Photocopiable

Who is broken?

Cut along the dotted lines. Glue the sections together to find a nursery rhyme character.

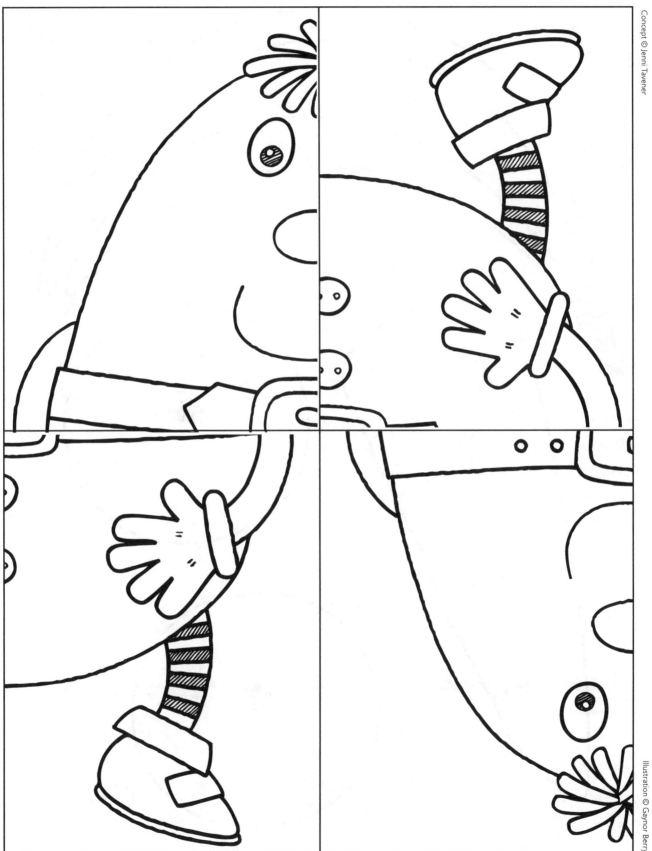

Photocopiable

Fruit face

Cut out the fruit. Stick them on to a paper plate to make a fruity face.

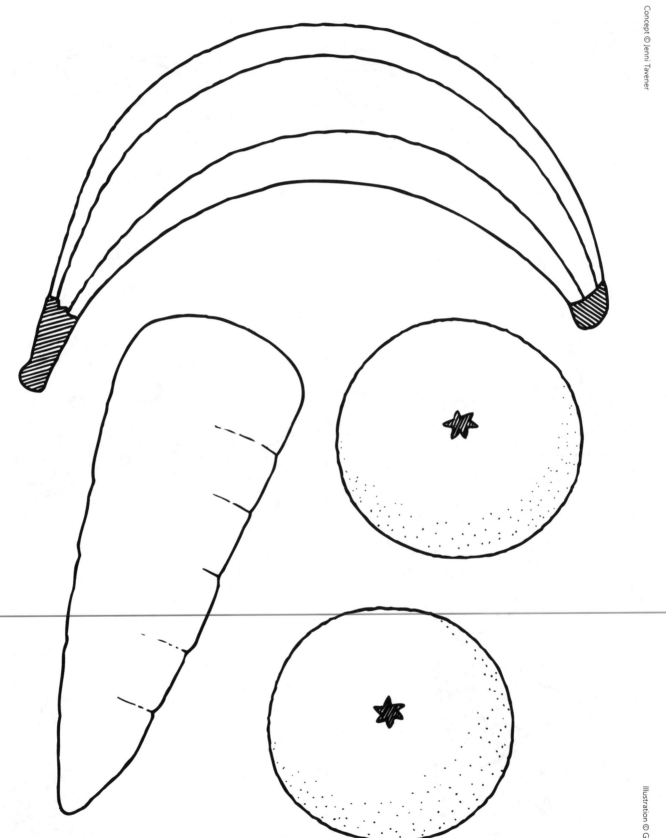

Photocopiable

Chapter 5

Templates

This chapter contains useful, time-saving templates that can be integrated into your day-to-day activities in a wide variety of ways. Use them to support your themed work or on their own for guessing, story-telling and matching games.

Can we help?

Colour in the pictures. Cut them out and use them for a guessing game.

Photocopiable

Minibeast templates

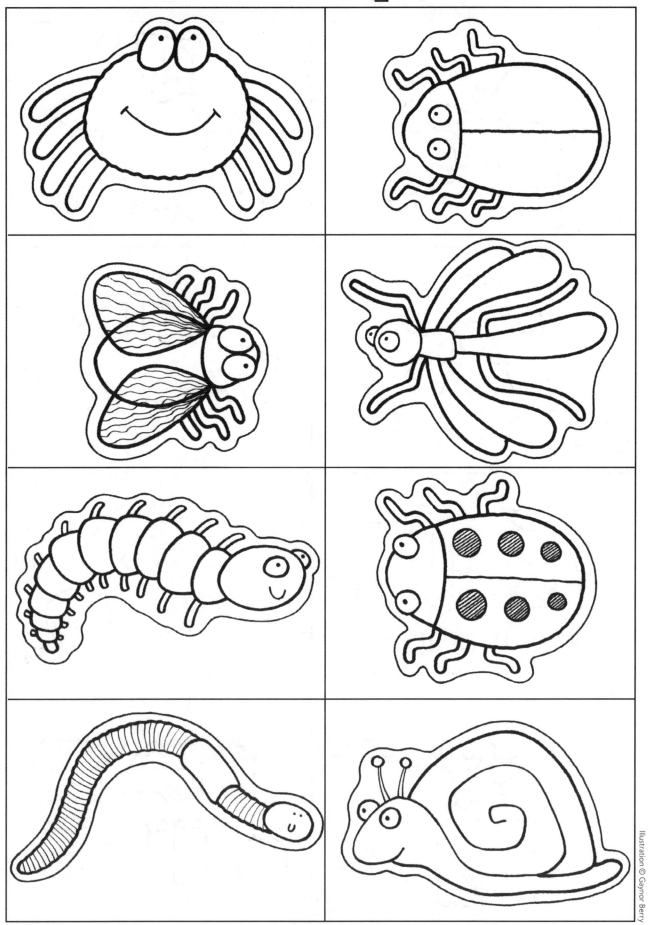

Illustration © Gaynor Berry

Photocopiable

Toy templates

Photocopiable

Character cut-outs

Cut out these pictures and use them to tell a story about Jack and the beanstalk.

Photocopiable

Illustrator © Gaynor Berry